TEAM SPIRIT®

SMART BOOKS FOR YOUNG FANS

THE CINCINNATI BENGALS

BY
MARK STEWART

New Hanover County Public Library
201 Chestnut Street
Wilmington, North Carolina 28401

NORWOOD HOUSE PRESS

CHICAGO, ILLINOIS

Norwood House Press
P.O. Box 316598
Chicago, Illinois 60631

For information regarding Norwood House Press, please visit our website at:
www.norwoodhousepress.com or call 866-565-2900.

All photos courtesy of Getty Images except the following:
Icon SMI (4), Topps, Inc. (6, 11, 15, 20, 34 left, 35 top right, 37, 40, 42 bottom left, 43 top),
Black Book Partners (8, 9, 10, 19, 22, 23, 27, 35 top left & bottom right, 38, 41, 45),
Tom DiPace (14), Cincinnati Bengals/NFL (21, 31, 43 bottom), Washington Redskins/NFL (28),
Author's Collection (33, 42 top left), NFLPA/Wonderful World (36), Matt Richman (48).
Cover Photo: Icon SMI

The memorabilia and artifacts pictured in this book are presented for educational and informational purposes,
and come from the collection of the author.

Editor: Mike Kennedy
Designer: Ron Jaffe
Project Management: Black Book Partners, LLC.
Special thanks to Topps, Inc.

Library of Congress Cataloging-in-Publication Data

Stewart, Mark, 1960-
  The Cincinnati Bengals / by Mark Stewart.
    p. cm. -- (Team spirit)
  Includes bibliographical references and index.
  Summary: "A revised Team Spirit Football edition featuring the Cincinnati
Bengals that chronicles the history and accomplishments of the team.
Includes access to the Team Spirit website which provides additional
information and photos"--Provided by publisher.
  ISBN 978-1-59953-518-0 (library edition : alk. paper) -- ISBN
978-1-60357-460-0 (ebook)
  1. Cincinnati Bengals (Football team)--History--Juvenile literature. I.
Title.
  GV956.C54S84 2012
  796.332'640977178--dc23
                                        2012014325

Manufactured in the United States of America in North Mankato, Minnesota.
205N—082012

COVER PHOTO: The Bengals celebrate a touchdown during the 2010 season.

Table of Contents

ABOUT OUR GLOSSARY

In this book, there may be several words that you are reading for the first time. Some are sports words, some are new vocabulary words, and some are familiar words that are used in an unusual way. All of these words are defined on page 46. Throughout the book, sports words appear in **bold type**. Regular vocabulary words appear in *bold italic type*.

Meet the Bengals

When football fans talk about the game's most talented teams, they usually focus on clubs that have one or two superstars who lead the way. The Cincinnati Bengals have had amazing talent over the years, yet they have never relied on a single star to lead them. Football is a team game, and that is how the Bengals have always played it. Every player is expected to contribute to Cincinnati's success.

When the Bengals take the field, they play like tigers. They follow their prey with great skill and wait for the right moment to strike. When the Bengals see an opportunity, they move quickly and attack with power.

This book tells the story of the Bengals. The team was started by one of the most brilliant men in *professional* football. The Bengals try to live up to his example every game. That is when the tiger in every player comes out.

Jermaine Gresham gets a hug from a teammate after a touchdown. The Bengals look for players who can score from anywhere on the field.

Glory Days

In the years after *World War II*, Paul Brown did more to change professional football than anyone else. He was the first coach to scout and sign African-American players, hire a full-time staff of assistant coaches, and make sure his team studied film of opposing teams. Not surprisingly, his Cleveland Browns won three **National Football League (NFL)** championships.

When Brown retired, he thought he would enjoy himself, but he soon became bored. In 1967—the same year that Brown was elected to the **Hall of Fame**—the **American Football League (AFL)** allowed him to start a new team in Cincinnati, Ohio. He named the team the Bengals and got busy finding players for the 1968 season.

Brown built his roster with unwanted players from other clubs. He also made smart picks in the **draft**. One of those selections was Paul Robinson. In Cincinnati's first season, he led the AFL in rushing with 1,023 yards and was named **Rookie of the Year**.

In 1970, the Bengals and the rest of the AFL teams became part of the NFL. By then, the Bengals had some of the best young players in the game, including Bob Trumpy, Bill Bergey, Ken Riley, Lemar Parrish, Mike Reid, and Horst Muhlmann. Cincinnati won the **Central Division** of the **American Football Conference (AFC)** with an 8 6 record. Brown was named Coach of the Year. He retired four seasons later.

Cincinnati had to look for new leaders. Quarterback Ken Anderson guided the team on the field for 12 seasons starting in 1972. He had a strong, accurate arm and knew how to get the best out of his teammates. His weapons included running backs Archie Griffin and Pete Johnson—two college stars from nearby Ohio State University—and receivers Isaac Curtis and Dan Ross.

In 1981, after three last-place finishes in a row, the Bengals rose to the top of the AFC. The team's coach was Forrest Gregg. He knew all about championship football. Gregg had been an offensive

LEFT: Paul Robinson
ABOVE: Ken Anderson

lineman for the Green Bay Packers in 1960s when they ruled the NFL. He led the Bengals to **Super Bowl** XVI, but they came up short of a victory against the San Francisco 49ers.

New stars joined the Bengals in the 1980s. David Fulcher and Tim Krumrie were the leaders of a tough defense. Cincinnati was even better on offense. Max Montoya and Anthony Munoz *anchored* the offensive line. Quarterback Boomer Esiason put points on the scoreboard with help from running back James Brooks and receivers Cris Collinsworth and Eddie Brown.

The Bengals won the AFC championship in 1988. Esiason had a great season and was named the league's **Most Valuable Player (MVP)**. The Bengals faced the 49ers again in the Super Bowl. Unfortunately, Cincinnati lost another close game.

The 1990s were not nearly as much fun for the Bengals and their fans. Outside of one season, the team had a losing record every year. Cincinnati tried to rebuild around stars such as Carl Pickens, Jeff Blake, and Corey Dillon, but the Bengals continued to struggle.

LEFT: Boomer Esiason
ABOVE: Corey Dillon

Things began to change when Marvin Lewis was hired as head coach in 2003. The Bengals finished at 8–8 in his first year. Two seasons later, Cincinnati won 11 games and made it back to the **playoffs** for the first time in 15 years. Lewis relied on a group of talented offensive players, including quarterback Carson Palmer, running back Rudi Johnson, and receivers Chad Ochocinco and T.J. Houshmandzadeh. Almost overnight, the Bengals became one of the NFL's most dangerous teams.

Many people thought the Bengals were on their way back to the Super Bowl in 2005. Johnson ran for 1,458 yards and 12 touchdowns. Ochocinco and Houshmandzadeh combined to catch 175 passes for 2,388 yards. Palmer had an amazing year with 32 touchdown passes.

Sadly, all of the championship dreams disappeared in the playoffs against the Pittsburgh Steelers. On the second play of the game, Palmer injured his knee and did not return. The Bengals lost 31–17.

The Bengals returned to the playoffs in 2009 after another remarkable season. They "swept" their division by winning every game against the Browns, Steelers, and Baltimore Ravens. Palmer and Ochocinco were still going strong, while Cedric Benson handled most of the rushing duties. Lewis was named Coach of the Year.

As age and injuries slowed down the team, Lewis faced the challenge of rebuilding the Bengals in 2011. He turned to a group of young players. Geno Atkins, Jermaine Gresham, A.J. Green, and Andy Dalton led the way. To the delight and surprise of Cincinnati fans, the team made it back to the playoffs. The Bengals started a new path to their first NFL championship.

LEFT: Chad Ochocinco
ABOVE: A.J. Green

Home Turf

For most of their history, the Bengals shared a stadium with another team. First it was Nippert Stadium, which was the home field of the University of Cincinnati Bearcats. In 1970, the team moved into Riverfront Stadium. It was built for the Cincinnati Reds baseball team.

In 2000, the Bengals finally got a home of their own when they opened Paul Brown Stadium. Cincinnati fans call it the "Jungle." On game days, they get loud and excited, which makes playing the Bengals a "wild" experience. A survey once ranked the stadium as one of America's favorite structures. It was the only football stadium that made the list.

BY THE NUMBERS

- The Bengals' stadium has 65,535 seats.
- At its tallest point, the stadium stands 157 feet high.
- There are more than 8,000 trees and shrubs planted around the stadium.

Cincinnati fans show their team spirit at the Bengals' stadium.

Dressed for Success

Cincinnati's colors are black, orange, and white—the same as a Bengal tiger's. During the 1960s and 1970s, the team used basic uniforms. For home games, the players' pants were white and their jerseys were black. The team's helmets were not very fancy, either. They were orange with *Bengals* spelled out in black letters.

How did the Bengals decide on their name? Paul Brown chose it in 1967. An earlier pro team that played in Cincinnati had been called the Bengals. Brown liked it and wanted to continue the **tradition**.

In 1981, the Bengals changed their look

KEN RILEY

CORNERBACK
BENGALS

by adding tiger stripes to their helmet. In 1997, they added a tiger *logo* to their jersey. In 2004, the team introduced new jerseys, which included a mostly orange style.

LEFT: Andy Dalton wears the team's 2011 home uniform.
RIGHT: This trading card shows Ken Riley in the uniform from the early 1970s.

We Won!

The Bengals have had some great teams over the years. They won the AFC championship twice in the 1980s. The team made an amazing turnaround in 1981 after finishing in last place the year before. The man who led Cincinnati was quarterback Ken Anderson. But in the season's first month, he struggled to find his rhythm, and the fans booed him. Once the Bengals got their timing on offense, the passing game came around.

Anderson used quick, short passes to pick apart opposing defenses. His favorite targets were Dan Ross, Isaac Curtis, Cris Collinsworth, and Steve Kreider. When the Bengals needed tough yards on the ground, Anderson handed the ball to burly Pete Johnson. He smashed into the line behind Anthony Munoz, Max Montoya, and Blair Bush. By the end of the year, the Bengals had the most wins in the AFC, Johnson had 16 touchdowns, and Anderson was the conference's top-ranked passer.

LEFT: Ken Anderson
RIGHT: Cris Collinsworth

The Bengals continued to roll in the playoffs. They won a close game against the Buffalo Bills on a late touchdown. The game was tied 21–21 in the fourth quarter when Anderson threw a scoring pass to Collinsworth. It was the first **postseason** victory in team history.

One week later, the Bengals hosted the San Diego Chargers for the AFC championship. The temperature was so cold that the game was nearly **postponed** for the safety of the players and fans. At kickoff, the temperature was 11 degrees below zero. With the wind, it felt even colder.

The Bengals adjusted to the bitter weather, and the Chargers did not. Anderson completed passes to seven different receivers. San Diego's Dan Fouts threw two **interceptions** deep in Cincinnati territory. When the clock ran out on the "Freezer Bowl," the Bengals celebrated a 27–7 victory. For the first time in team history, they were AFC champions.

In Super Bowl XVI, Cincinnati faced the San Francisco 49ers. Both teams were looking for their first NFL title. The Bengals gained more yards than the 49ers, but it was San Francisco that built a big lead. Cincinnati fought back in the second half only to lose 26–21. Ross set a Super Bowl record with 11 receptions.

The Bengals went from worst to first again in 1988. This time, Boomer Esiason was the team's quarterback. Like Anderson, he was a talented star with an accurate arm. Esiason finished the season as the AFC's top-ranked passer. The running attack was terrific, too. A rookie named Ickey Woods ran hard all year long and led the conference with 15 touchdowns. He combined with lightning-fast James Brooks to rush for 1,997 yards.

Cincinnati opened the playoffs against the Seattle Seahawks. The Bengals scored three touchdowns early in the game. They controlled the action the rest of the way and held on for a 21–13 victory.

Next, the Bengals faced the Bills for the AFC championship. The Cincinnati defense was superb. The Bills gained just 181 yards. The Bengals held Buffalo superstar Thurman Thomas to a total of six yards for the entire game! Meanwhile, Woods ran the ball 29 times and wore out the Buffalo defense. The Bengals went on to win 21–10 and capture their second conference title.

In Super Bowl XXIII, the Bengals again played the 49ers. It was another close game. Cincinnati led by three points late in the fourth quarter. Unfortunately, San Francisco quarterback Joe Montana had a miracle left in his right arm. The 49ers scored the game-winning touchdown

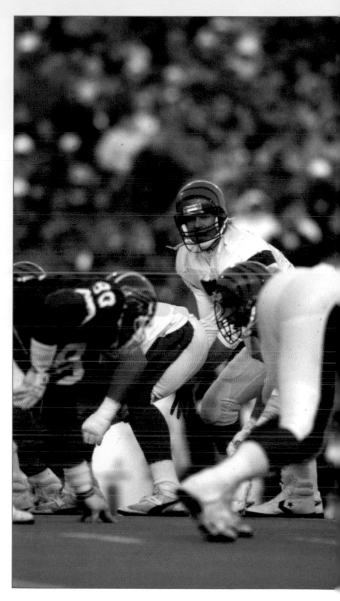

with 34 seconds left. It was a disappointing loss for Cincinnati, but the fans took a lot of pride in knowing that the team that beat them was one of the greatest in history.

LEFT: Ickey Woods celebrates a touchdown with his famous dance, the "Ickey Shuffle."   **ABOVE**: Boomer Esiason looks over the Buffalo defense as he barks out signals.

Go-To Guys

To be a true star in the NFL, you need more than fast feet and a big body. You have to be a "go-to guy"—someone the coach wants on the field at the end of a big game. Bengals fans have had a lot to cheer about over the years, including these great stars ...

THE PIONEERS

BENGALS AFC
TIGHT END
BOB TRUMPY

BOB TRUMPY   Tight End

- BORN: 3/6/1945   • PLAYED FOR TEAM: 1968 TO 1977

Bob Trumpy was quick and strong, and he had very soft hands. That was the perfect combination for a tight end. He played in the **Pro Bowl** in each of his first three seasons.

BOB JOHNSON   Offensive Lineman

- BORN: 8/19/1946   • PLAYED FOR TEAM: 1968 TO 1979

Bob Johnson was the first player drafted by the Bengals in 1968. In 1979, he was the last of the original Bengals. Johnson played center and was one of the NFL's best blockers. He was Cincinnati's radio announcer when the team went to its first Super Bowl.

KEN RILEY   Defensive Back

- BORN: 8/6/1947   • PLAYED FOR TEAM: 1969 TO 1983

Ken Riley was a brilliant student and an excellent quarterback in college. When Riley joined the Bengals, coach Paul Brown decided he would make a great safety. When Riley retired, only three players in history had more interceptions.

LEMAR PARRISH   Defensive Back

- BORN: 12/13/1947   • PLAYED FOR TEAM: 1970 TO 1977

Lemar Parrish was one of the most fearless cornerbacks in football. He covered some of the best receivers in the NFL and was not afraid to tackle players who outweighed him by 50 pounds.

KEN ANDERSON   Quarterback

- BORN: 2/15/1949   • PLAYED FOR TEAM: 1971 TO 1986

Ken Anderson was the NFL's top-ranked passer four times. He and assistant coach Bill Walsh worked together to create an unstoppable passing attack. Anderson was named the NFL MVP after the 1981 season.

ISAAC CURTIS   Receiver

- BORN: 10/20/1950
- PLAYED FOR TEAM: 1973 TO 1984

No receiver scared NFL defenses more than Isaac Curtis. He could find an open space anywhere on the field and specialized in catching long passes. Curtis was voted an **All-Pro** four times.

LEFT: Bob Trumpy   **RIGHT**: Isaac Curtis

ANTHONY MUNOZ   Offensive Lineman

• BORN: 8/19/1958   • PLAYED FOR TEAM: 1980 TO 1992

Anthony Munoz fought through injury problems in college to become one of the NFL's best offensive linemen during the 1980s. He was named to the Pro Bowl 11 times and entered the Hall of Fame in 1998.

CRIS COLLINSWORTH   Receiver

• BORN: 1/27/1959   • PLAYED FOR TEAM: 1981 TO 1988

Cris Collinsworth looked too tall and skinny to make it in the NFL. But no receiver in the league was tougher, and no one gave a better effort play after play after play. Collinsworth was as dangerous on short pass routes as he was on long bombs.

BOOMER ESIASON   Quarterback

• BORN: 4/17/1961   • PLAYED FOR TEAM: 1984 TO 1992 & 1997

Boomer Esiason was a great leader who loved to throw the football. Esiason led the AFC in touchdown passes twice and was the NFL MVP in 1988.

WILLIE ANDERSON   Offensive Lineman

• BORN: 7/11/1975   • PLAYED FOR TEAM: 1996 TO 2007

Willie Anderson was one of the biggest and strongest players in the NFL. At 340 pounds, he was also quick and *agile*. Anderson opened huge holes for his running backs and kept his quarterback safe from **sacks**.

CHAD OCHOCINCO
Receiver

- BORN: 1/9/1978
- PLAYED FOR TEAM: 2001 TO 2010

Chad Ochocinco was an All-Pro three times for the Bengals. In 2006, he set an NFL record with 450 receiving yards over back-to-back games. That year he legally changed his last name from Johnson to Ochocinco. In Spanish, "ocho cinco" means "8–5," which was the number he wore.

CEDRIC BENSON
Running Back

- BORN: 12/28/1982
- FIRST YEAR WITH TEAM: 2008

Cedric Benson became Cincinnati's starting running back midway through the 2008 season. He topped 1,000 yards each year from 2009 to 2011. Benson had an intestinal illness called celiac disease. In order to play, he had to eat a special *gluten-free* diet.

A.J. GREEN
Receiver

- BORN: 7/31/1988
- FIRST YEAR WITH TEAM: 2011

The Bengals used the fourth pick in the 2011 draft to select A.J. Green. The speedy and athletic receiver didn't disappoint them. As a rookie, he averaged 16 yards per catch and played in the Pro Bowl.

LEFT: Anthony Munoz
ABOVE: Chad Ochocinco

Calling the Shots

f you had to pick one person to start a football team, you couldn't do better than Paul Brown. No one had a keener eye for talent. In fact, when Brown began building the Bengals in 1968, the other AFL teams were afraid to do business with him. They were sure he would find players on their rosters that were diamonds in the rough.

Brown also had a good feel for hiring young assistant coaches. In fact, some of football's greatest leaders got their start with Brown—including Chuck Noll, Don Shula, and Bill Walsh. One of Cincinnati's first quarterbacks, Sam Wyche, later became one of the team's best coaches.

Brown led the Bengals to the playoffs in 1970 and again in 1973 and 1975. In 1976, he stepped aside as coach and continued to guide the team as its owner. The super-serious Brown relaxed a little in his new role. Once, reporters asked him about the "Ickey Shuffle," the touchdown dance performed by Ickey Woods. The 80-year-old Brown said he liked it—and then did his own version of the dance!

The first coach to lead the Bengals to the Super Bowl was Forrest Gregg. He taught his players how to work together as one. Wyche

Paul Brown talks things over with Sam Wyche. The Cincinnati quarterback later became the team's coach.

also guided the Bengals to the Super Bowl. He was best known for his no-huddle offense. Wyche believed that a smart quarterback could call plays as he scanned the defense at the **line of scrimmage**, which kept opponents off balance.

In 2003, the Bengals hired Marvin Lewis as head coach. He was one of the first African Americans to rise to this position in the NFL. Lewis specialized in building strong defenses. He turned the Bengals into one of the NFL's toughest teams. In 2011, Lewis passed Wyche for the most career victories by a Cincinnati coach.

One Great Day

The old saying "records are made to be broken" is definitely true in pro football. Every season players get bigger, faster, stronger, and better—and more records fall. Still, there are a handful of records that stand the test of time. The mark for most rushing yards in a game by a rookie seemed to be one of them. In 1957, first-year star Jim Brown rumbled for 237 yards. That record stood unchallenged for more than three decades.

When the Bengals took the field for a Thursday night game late in the 1997 season, Corey Dillon was tearing up AFC defenses. Though he started the year on the bench, the rookie was on pace to top 1,000 yards. Still, no one expected him to do much against the Tennessee Oilers (who had not yet changed their name to the Titans). They had one of the league's best defenses against the run.

The Bengals were coming to the end of a disappointing season. They would finish with a record of 7–9 and miss the playoffs for the seventh year in a row. Dillon was one of the team's few bright spots. In

Corey Dillon celebrates a touchdown.

his first five games as a starter, Dillon ran for exactly 500 yards.

The Oilers knew that Cincinnati would hand the ball to Dillon again and again. The rookie knew they were waiting for him. From the first time Dillon touched the ball, it was clear that Tennessee had **underestimated** him. He exploded through tacklers for one big gain after another. Dillon scored three touchdowns in the first half and a fourth in the third quarter. The Bengals built a huge lead, 38–0.

To win, all Cincinnati needed to do was run out the clock. Dillon kept piling up yards. In the fourth quarter, he beat the team record of 201 yards set by James Brooks. But Dillon wasn't done. He finished with 246 yards on 39 carries to shatter Brown's mark. After the game, one of the Tennessee defenders put it best: "If you break one of Jim Brown's records, you deserve all the credit you can get."

Legend Has It

LEGEND HAS IT that Coy Bacon did. Bacon played just two years for the Bengals, but no Cincinnati player was ever better at getting to the quarterback. According to the team, Bacon had 22 sacks in 1976—more than anyone else in the NFL. Sacks, however, were not an official statistic back then. In 2001, Michael Strahan of the New York Giants had 22.5 sacks. Unfortunately, Bacon's name never made it into the record books. But he will always be remembered as Cincinnati's most feared pass-rusher.

ABOVE: Coy Bacon

What was Cincinnati's most famous kick?

LEGEND HAS IT that it was a missed **extra point**. During Sam Wyche's time as Cincinnati's coach, he had a red-hot *rivalry* with coach Jerry Glanville. Nothing gave Wyche more pleasure than watching Glanville squirm on the sidelines. In a 1989 game, the Bengals demolished Glanville's Houston Oilers, 61–7. It would have been 62–7, but Cincinnati kicker Lee Johnson missed an extra point. After the huge victory, reporters asked Wyche if he was sorry for running up the score. "Our only real regret is that Johnson missed that extra point," he said.

Did the Bengals make the biggest turnaround in NFL history?

LEGEND HAS IT that they did. In 1987, Cincinnati could do nothing right. The Bengals won just four games. Many of their losses came on strange and unexpected plays. The fans were ready to give up on the team. One season later, in 1988, the same players performed like superstars. Boomer Esiason was the best quarterback in the NFL, and Ickey Woods ran for more than 1,000 yards. The Bengals completed their incredible turnaround by making it all the way to the Super Bowl.

Cincinnati fans are used to bundling up for games. When the winter winds whip down from Canada, southern Ohio can feel like the North Pole. Still, no one expected the temperature to drop so low for Cincinnati's first **AFC Championship Game**. The Bengals hosted the San Diego Chargers for the right to go to Super Bowl XVI.

At kickoff, the thermometer read 11 degrees below zero. The wind was blowing steadily around 35 miles per hour. No one could ever remember such a bitterly cold day. A week earlier, the Chargers had beaten the Miami Dolphins in a playoff game. The weather had been so warm and muggy that many players needed oxygen on the field. When the Chargers walked onto the frigid field in Cincinnati, they already looked like a beaten team. The cold was too much for them.

The Bengals loved the conditions. They sent a message to the Chargers by taking the field without wearing long-sleeve shirts. San Diego's players knew they were in for a battle.

The Bengals scored first on a field goal. Then, after a **fumble** by the Chargers, Cincinnati moved ahead 10–0. The Chargers fought back, but Louis Breeden stopped their rally with an interception. Moments later, Pete Johnson barreled over the goal line to make the score 17–7.

In the second half, the Bengals took full control. The Chargers were helpless against the Cincinnati defense. When the final gun sounded, the Bengals celebrated their 27–7 victory. They won the AFC crown for the first time in team history—and fans would always remember the game as the "Freezer Bowl."

Team Spirit

When opposing teams play in Cincinnati, they have to be ready for the Bengals—and their fans. The people in the stands know their football, and they know how to make a lot of noise when the Bengals need a boost. In the 1980s, they started calling their stadium the Jungle. They took the name with them when they moved to a new stadium in 2000. During games, the team likes to play an old rock song called "Welcome to the Jungle." The crowd always goes wild, and the Bengals feed off that energy.

Another tradition that started in the 1980s was a funny cheer known as "Who Dey." Fans in one part of the stadium shout, "Who dey think gonna beat them Bengals?" Fans in another part of the stadium reply, "Nobody!" The Bengals kept that chant in mind when they named their friendly, fluffy tiger mascot. He's known as Who Dey, and the fans love him.

LEFT: Team spirit knows no limit at Bengals games.
ABOVE: This pin celebrates the team's trip to the Super Bowl in 1989.

Timeline

In this timeline, each Super Bowl is listed under the year it was played. Remember that the Super Bowl is held early in the year and is actually part of the previous season. For example, Super Bowl XLVI was played on February 5, 2012, but it was the championship of the 2011 NFL season.

1968
The Bengals play their first season.

1975
Ken Anderson is the AFC's top-ranked passer for the second year in a row.

1970
The team finishes first in the AFC Central.

1982
The Bengals reach the Super Bowl for the first time.

1989
The Bengals return to the Super Bowl.

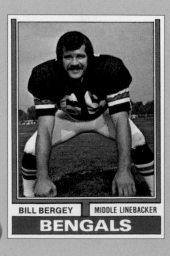

Bill Bergey was the leader of the defense in the 1970s.

Forrest Gregg coached the team to the Super Bowl in 1982.

Jeff
Blake

T.J.
Houshmandzadeh

1995
Jeff Blake leads the AFC
with 28 touchdown passes.

2007
T.J. Houshmandzadeh leads
the NFL with 112 catches.

1996
Carl Pickens leads the
AFC with 100 catches.

2004
Rudi Johnson is voted
to the Pro Bowl.

2011
Andy Dalton throws
20 touchdown passes
as a rookie.

Carl
Pickens

Rudi
Johnson

Fun Facts

MUSIC MAN

In 1975, star lineman Mike Reid left the Bengals to become a professional musician. He toured the country giving piano concerts and later won a *Grammy Award* in 1984 for writing the song "Stranger in the House." Reid is in the College Football Hall of Fame and also the Nashville Songwriters Hall of Fame.

RECORD SETTER

After setting an NFL mark for most yards by a rookie in 1997, Corey Dillon went right on smashing records. In 2000, he set a league record with 278 yards in a game. In 2001, he set a team record with a 96-yard touchdown run.

LONG WAIT

A.J. Green was voted to the 2012 Pro Bowl. The last Cincinnati receiver to earn this honor as a rookie was Cris Collinsworth, in 1981.

ABOVE: Mike Reid   **RIGHT**: Tim Krumrie

MAN OF STEEL

After shattering his leg in Super Bowl XXIII, Tim Krumie had a 15-inch steel rod implanted next to the bone to keep it safe. Instead of retiring, Krumrie returned to the NFL and played for six more years. He led the Bengals in tackles in 1992.

TIM KRUMRIE

NT

LIKE FATHER, LIKE SON

In 2011, Geno Atkins became a star in his second season in Cincinnati. No defensive tackle in football had more sacks. He learned the game from his father. Gene Atkins was an NFL safety for 10 seasons.

BAT MAN

If Cedric Benson hadn't become a star running back for the Bengals, he could always have gone back to baseball. Benson was drafted by the Los Angeles Dodgers in high school and actually played a few games as a pro before deciding to stick with football.

WEBB MASTERS

In 1981, the Bengals had one of the best defensive lines in football. Fans nicknamed the group "The WEBB"—after the last-name initials of Wilson Whitley, Eddie Edwards, Gary Burley, and Ross Browner.

Talking Football

"When you're a quarterback, you're either the bum or the hero."
► *Carson Palmer, on the good and bad of being a team leader*

"Sometimes you're thankful your heart doesn't come out through your chest!"
► *Anthony Munoz, on how excited he would get before each snap*

"I just told our players how proud I am of them and we are of each other. We didn't do anything wrong. The 49ers played a great game."
► *Sam Wyche, on Cincinnati's narrow defeat in Super Bowl XXIII*

"When you win, say nothing. When you lose, say less."
► *Paul Brown, on playing with class*

"There's no substitute for a scoreboard. You either won or you lost."

▶ **Cris Collinsworth**, *on the way success and failure are measured in the NFL*

"You have to learn not to take any unnecessary chances. It's just stupid for any of us quarterbacks to try and take on 265-pound linebackers."

▶ **Boomer Esiason**, *on helping the team by staying healthy*

"I've been able to do a lot and have been given some great opportunities, but I feel like it's just the beginning."

▶ **Andy Dalton**, *on starting all 16 games as a rookie quarterback in 2011*

"Everybody says, 'He's always talking.' But out on the field I'm walking the walk every Sunday."

▶ **Chad Ochocinco**, *on the thrill of gamedays*

LEFT: Carson Palmer
ABOVE: Cris Collinsworth

Great Debates

People who root for the Bengals love to compare their favorite moments, teams, and players. Some debates have been going on for years! How would you settle these classic football arguments?

The 1981 Bengals would beat the 1988 Bengals ...

... because they had so many weapons. Ken Anderson almost never threw a bad pass. He and his receivers—Dan Ross, Cris Collinsworth, and Isaac Curtis—would have picked the 1988 Bengals apart. Then there was Pete Johnson. He ran like a bulldozer and also caught 46 passes that year. On defense, Ken Riley and Louis Breeden would have had no trouble covering the 1988 receivers—even though one of them was Collinsworth!

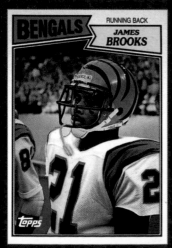

Sorry. The 1988 Bengals win this one ...

... because when it comes to weapons, they had the clear edge. Boomer Esiason threw for more than 3,500 yards. Ickey Woods and James Brooks ( ) combined to run the ball for nearly 2,000 yards. And, five Bengals had 20 or more catches. The defense was just as good. The 1988 Bengals were dangerous on both sides of the ball.

Boomer Esiason was the Bengals' greatest quarterback ...

… because he was so good at running the team's no-huddle offense. Esiason (   ) was a master at reading defenses and spotting opportunities for big plays. Also, no one was ever better at faking handoffs. Esiason made the defense think he had given the ball to a teammate, and then like magic he was throwing a pass to a receiver. The "play-action pass" became the main weapon in Cincinnati's attack.

Seriously? Ken Anderson was the team's best passer ...

… because he turned the Bengals into a championship contender. Anderson was the first quarterback to truly master the short passing game. But he could also throw the ball long when the defense crowded the line of scrimmage. Anderson was the league's top-rated passer four times and led the NFL in passing yards twice.

For the Record

The great Bengals teams and players have left their marks on the record books. These are the "best of the best" …

Paul Brown

BENGALS AWARD WINNERS

WINNER	AWARD	YEAR
Paul Robinson	AFL Rookie of the Year	1968
Paul Brown	AFL Coach of the Year	1969
Greg Cook	AFL Rookie of the Year	1969
Paul Brown	AFL Coach of the Year	1970
Ken Anderson	NFL MVP	1981
Ken Anderson	NFL Comeback Player of the Year	1981
Eddie Brown	NFL Offensive Rookie of the Year	1985
Boomer Esiason	NFL MVP	1988
Jon Kitna	NFL Comeback Player of the Year	2003
Carson Palmer	Pro Bowl MVP	2007
Marvin Lewis	NFL Coach of the Year	2009

Eddie Brown

Jon Kitna

BENGALS ACHIEVEMENTS

ACHIEVEMENT	YEAR
AFC Central Champions	1970
AFC Central Champions	1973
AFC Central Champions	1981
AFC Champions	1981
AFC Central Champions	1988
AFC Champions	1988
AFC Central Champions	1990
AFC North Champions	2005
AFC North Champions	2009

Greg Cook

ABOVE: Greg Cook was Rookie of the Year in 1969.
LEFT: Ross Browner was the defensive star of the 1981 team.

Pinpoints

The history of a football team is made up of many smaller stories. These stories take place all over the map—not just in the city a team calls "home." Match the pushpins on these maps to the **Team Facts**, and you will begin to see the story of the Bengals unfold!

TEAM FACTS

1 Cincinnati, Ohio—*The team has played here since 1968.*

2 Miami, Florida—*The Bengals played in Super Bowl XXIII here.*

3 Springfield, Illinois—*Bob Trumpy was born here.*

4 Victorville, California—*T.J. Houshmandzadeh was born here.*

5 Birthright, Texas—*Forrest Gregg was born here.*

6 Ardmore, Oklahoma—*Jermaine Gresham was born here.*

7 West Islip, New York—*Boomer Esiason was born here.*

8 Fort Valley, Georgia—*Pete Johnson was born here.*

9 Petersburg, Virginia—*Rudi Johnson was born here.*

10 Murphy, North Carolina—*Carl Pickens was born here.*

11 Pontiac, Michigan—*The Bengals played in Super Bowl XVI here.*

12 Dortmund, Germany—*Horst Muhlmann was born here.*

Rudi Johnson

12

AFC CHAMPIONSHIP GAME—The game played to determine which AFC team will go to the Super Bowl.

AGILE—Quick and graceful.

ALL-PRO—An honor given to the best players at their positions at the end of each season.

AMERICAN FOOTBALL CONFERENCE (AFC)—One of two groups of teams that make up the NFL.

AMERICAN FOOTBALL LEAGUE (AFL)—The football league that began play in 1960 and later merged with the NFL.

ANCHORED—Held steady.

CENTRAL DIVISION—A group of teams that play in the central part of the country.

DRAFT—The annual meeting at which teams choose from the best college players.

EXTRA POINT—A kick worth one point, attempted after a touchdown.

FUMBLE—A ball that is dropped by the player carrying it.

GLUTEN-FREE—Without proteins found in wheat and other grains.

GRAMMY AWARD—An honor given to people in the music industry.

HALL OF FAME—The museum in Canton, Ohio, where football's greatest players are honored. Other sports and entertainment industries have similar museums.

INTERCEPTIONS—Passes that are caught by the defensive team.

LINE OF SCRIMMAGE—The imaginary line that separates the offense and defense before each play begins.

LOGO—A symbol or design that represents a company or team.

MOST VALUABLE PLAYER (MVP)—The award given each year to the league's best player; also given to the best player in the Super Bowl and Pro Bowl.

NATIONAL FOOTBALL LEAGUE (NFL)—The league that started in 1920 and is still operating today.

PLAYOFFS—The games played after the regular season to determine which teams play in the Super Bowl.

POSTPONED—Put off to a later time.

POSTSEASON—Another term for playoffs.

PRO BOWL—The NFL's all-star game, played after the regular season.

PROFESSIONAL—Paid to play.

RIVALRY—Extremely emotional competition.

ROOKIE OF THE YEAR—The annual award given to the league's best first-year player.

SACKS—Tackles of the quarterback behind the line of scrimmage.

SUPER BOWL—The championship of the NFL, played between the winners of the National Football Conference and American Football Conference.

TRADITION—A belief or custom that is handed down from generation to generation.

UNDERESTIMATED—Placed too low a value on.

WORLD WAR II—The war among the major powers of Europe, Asia, and North America that lasted from 1939 to 1945. The United States entered the war in 1941.

OVERTIME

TEAM SPIRIT introduces a great way to stay up to date with your team! Visit our **OVERTIME** link and get connected to the latest and greatest updates. **OVERTIME** serves as a young reader's ticket to an exclusive web page—with more stories, fun facts, team records, and photos of the Bengals. Content is updated during and after each season. The **OVERTIME** feature also enables readers to send comments and letters to the author! Log onto:

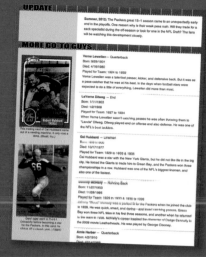

www.norwoodhousepress.com/library.aspx

and click on the tab: **TEAM SPIRIT** to access **OVERTIME**.

Read all the books in the series to learn more about professional sports. For a complete listing of the baseball, basketball, football, and hockey teams in the **TEAM SPIRIT** series, visit our website at:

www.norwoodhousepress.com/library.aspx

On the Road

CINCINNATI BENGALS
One Paul Brown Stadium
Cincinnati, Ohio 45202
513-621-3550
www.bengals.com

THE PRO FOOTBALL HALL OF FAME
2121 George Halas Drive NW
Canton, Ohio 44708
330-456-8207
www.profootballhof.com

On the Bookshelf

To learn more about the sport of football, look for these books at your library or bookstore:

• Frederick, Shane. *The Best of Everything Football Book*. North Mankato, Minnesota: Capstone Press, 2011.

• Jacobs, Greg. *The Everything Kids' Football Book: The All-Time Greats, Legendary Teams, Today's Superstars—And Tips on Playing Like a Pro*. Avon, Massachusetts: Adams Media Corporation, 2010.

• Editors of *Sports Illustrated for Kids*. *1st and 10: Top 10 Lists of Everything in Football*. New York, New York: Sports Illustrated Books, 2011.

Index

PAGE NUMBERS IN **BOLD** REFER TO ILLUSTRATIONS.

About the Author

MARK STEWART has written more than 50 books on football and over 150 sports books for kids. He grew up in New York City during the 1960s rooting for the Giants and Jets, and was lucky enough to meet players from both teams. Mark comes from a family of writers. His grandfather was Sunday Editor of *The New York Times,* and his mother was Articles Editor of *Ladies' Home Journal* and *McCall's*. Mark has profiled hundreds of athletes over the past 25 years. He has also written several books about his native New York and New Jersey, his home today. Mark is a graduate of Duke University, with a degree in history. He lives and works in a home overlooking Sandy Hook, New Jersey. You can contact Mark through the Norwood House Press website.